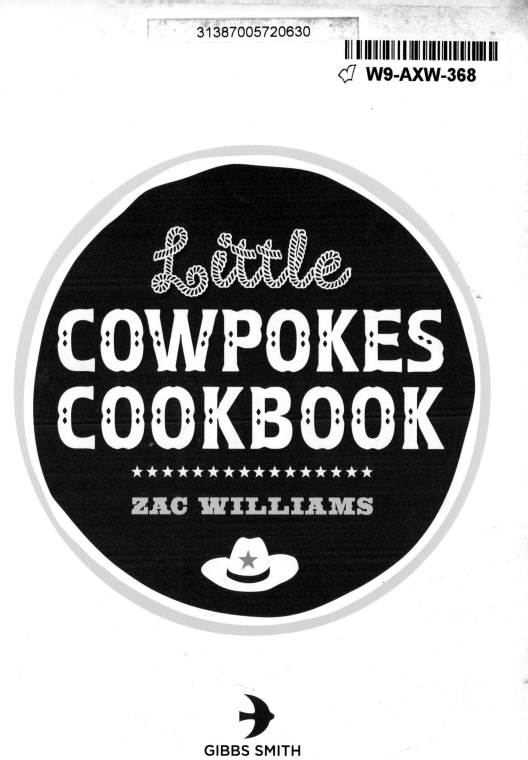

Little
COWPOKES
COOKBOOK

★★★★★★★★★★★★★★★

ZAC WILLIAMS

GIBBS SMITH
TO ENRICH AND INSPIRE HUMANKIND

For Grandma Betty, who taught me that imagination and food go hand in hand.

Manufactured in Shenzhen, China, in February 2013 by Toppan

The cooking and baking activities suggested in this book may involve the use of sharp objects and hot surfaces. Parental guidance is recommended. The author and publisher disclaim all responsibility of injury resulting from the performance of any activities listed in this book. Readers assume all legal responsibility for their actions.

First Edition
17 16 15 14 13   5 4 3 2 1

Published by
Gibbs Smith
P.O. Box 667
Layton, Utah 84041

1.800.835.4993 orders
www.gibbs-smith.com

Designed by Katie Jennings
Printed and bound in China

Gibbs Smith books are printed on either recycled, 100% post-consumer waste, FSC-certified papers or on paper produced from sustainable PEFC-certified forest/controlled wood source. Learn more at www.pefc.org.

Library of Congress Cataloging-in-Publication Data

Williams, Zac.
Little cowpokes cookbook / Zac Williams. -- First edition.
pages cm
ISBN 978-1-4236-3208-5
1. Cooking, American--Western style. I. Title.
TX715.2.W47W545 2013
641.5973--dc23
2012033100

Contents

A RECIPE ROUNDUP

So you're ready to saddle up and live the life of a cowpoke are ya'? Well, one of the most important skills a good range rider can have is to know how to whip up tasty vittles when called upon. This here collection of recipes is guaranteed to be just the ticket to delicious cooking. You won't be a tenderfoot for long, pilgrim, if you take my advice and master the skills of the cowboy kitchen.

Here are important rules to keep all junior bronc busters from getting hurt.

✶ Always ask an adult to help when using the stove, microwave or oven. To help avoid burns and fires, never use a cooking range or microwave without adult supervision.

✶ Knives can be very dangerous. Have a grown-up help you chop or cut any ingredients that require a sharp blade. Don't ever play with kitchen knives. They are tools for use in cooking only.

✶ Small kitchen appliances such as blenders and food processors help make cooking easier, but they should always be used with an adult's assistance. Never put utensils or hands into these appliances.

✶ Wash your hands with soap and warm water before beginning to cook and wash your hands often while cooking to keep germs out of what you are making.

✶ Make sure to properly refrigerate foods that can easily spoil such as meats, dairy products, eggs and other products. This avoids sickness from bacteria in the food.

✶ Never use the same plate that raw food has been for food that is ready to serve.

✶ Keep your kitchen work area clean and organized. Clean up spills quickly so you or someone else doesn't slip. Keep towels and other flammable items away from the stove.

✶ While sometimes you need a boost to reach the kitchen counter, be very careful to only stand on a safe stepping stool so you don't fall.

✶ And, most importantly, always ask for permission and help from a grown-up so they can make sure you have fun in the kitchen!

So let's ride 'em out and get cookin'!

Breakfast
AT THE RANCH

Life as a cowpoke is hard work. It means getting
up before sunrise to move cattle, mend fences,
and tend to the ranch work, while keeping
a sharp eye out for rustlers. A hearty breakfast
is important to keeping ranch hands happy
and working hard. To fuel up, enjoy a full table
spread with delicious dishes outdoors.

CH HOUSE BREAKFAST
own Sugar Mule Muffins
Huevos Rancheros
Flappin' Flap Jacks
Blueberry Sauce
Fruit Pony Tails
Cowboy Kettle Cocoa

BROWN SUGAR MULE MUFFINS

2 cups brown sugar

1 cup butter, softened

2 eggs, beaten

2 cups milk

4 cups flour

$1/2$ teaspoon salt

2 teaspoons vanilla

2 teaspoons baking soda

1. Preheat oven to 375 degrees F. Prepare mini muffin tins by spraying with cooking spray.

2. Mix together brown sugar and butter until creamy. Add eggs and milk, stirring to combine. While continuing to mix, stir in remaining ingredients.

3. Pour muffin batter into muffin tins, filling each cup about half full. Bake for 15–20 minutes until slightly browned. Serve in a basket with butter or jam as desired.

★ Makes about 48 mini muffins

EGGS RANCHEROS

1 dozen fresh eggs

$^1/_4$ cup milk

Salt to taste

Black pepper to taste

8 flour tortillas

1 tablespoon butter or margarine

1 cup shredded Mexican-style cheese

2 cups fresh salsa

1. In a mixing bowl, beat together eggs, milk, salt and pepper until well mixed.

2. Using cookie cutters shaped like stars, cowboy hats and horses, cut out shapes from the tortillas.

3. In a cast iron skillet over medium-high heat, melt butter. When the butter has melted, add the beaten egg mixture. For extra-fluffy eggs, wait a few minutes until the bottom is cooked and then gently fold the bottom of the eggs to the top using a spatula. Continue folding the bottom to the top, until the desired firmness is reached.

4. Stir in shredded cheese and serve in skillet with tortilla cutouts and fresh salsa.

★ Makes 8 servings

BUTTERMILK FLAPPIN' FLAPJACKS WITH BLUEBERRY SAUCE

3 cups all-purpose flour

3 tablespoons brown sugar

3 teaspoons baking powder

1½ teaspoons baking soda

¾ teaspoon salt

3 cups buttermilk

1 cup milk

3 eggs

⅓ cup butter, melted

1. In a large mixing bowl combine the first 5 dry ingredients. Using a fork, stir to combine. In a separate bowl, beat together the remaining 4 wet ingredients.

2. Preheat a lightly oiled griddle over medium-high heat (325 degrees F for electric griddle). If you drop water on the surface and it beads and sizzles, it's ready to cook.

3. Combine both mixtures and mix with a fork until just blended and no powdery mix remains. Don't over stir. Some lumps are okay. Using a ⅓ cup to measure, pour the batter onto the hot griddle. Cook a few minutes on each side. As bubbles pop on the edges, the flapjack is ready to turn over. Serve with hot Blueberry Sauce.

Blueberry Sauce

1 cup sugar

3 tablespoons cornstarch

1 cup water

4 cups frozen blueberries,
  thawed

Combine sugar, cornstarch
and water in a saucepan,
stirring well to mix. Add the
thawed blueberries and cook
over medium heat for about
10 minutes until the sauce is
thick and bubbling. Allow to
cool slightly and serve with
flapjacks while still warm.

★ Makes 8 servings of
   2–3 pancakes each

FRUIT PONY TAILS

1 honeydew melon

1 cantaloupe

1 small seedless watermelon

1 pint strawberries

1. Remove seeds from and cut the honeydew and cantaloupe into pieces about an inch square. Cut the watermelon in half and reserve one half. Cut the remaining half into about 1-inch squares. Wash and cut the tops off the strawberries.

2. Using bamboo skewers, make kabobs using the melon pieces and strawberries. Using the reserved half of the watermelon on a platter as a base, stick the fruit tails into the watermelon to serve.

★ Makes 8–12 servings

COWBOY KETTLE COCOA

$^1/_2$ cup cocoa

$1^1/_2$ cups sugar

$^2/_3$ cup hot water

8 cups milk ($^1/_2$ gallon)

$1^1/_2$ teaspoons vanilla

$^1/_4$ teaspoon cinnamon

Whipped cream

Dash nutmeg

1. In a large saucepan, combine cocoa, sugar and hot water. Over medium-high heat, bring to a boil, stirring well to mix. Add milk and continue to heat until hot. Do not boil.

2. Remove from heat and add vanilla and cinnamon. Serve in mugs topped with whipped cream and a dash of nutmeg.

★ Makes 8 generous servings

Cowpunchers
CAMPOUT

When you make your home on the range, it gets
kind of lonely. That's why it's always so nice
to have a little sagebrush get-together under the
stars. Invite a few of your pardners to cook over
a fire, play a little cards and sing some songs
while enjoying tasty campout bites.

RANGE BBQ CHICKEN

4 boneless, skinless chicken breasts
1 can lemon-lime soda
2 tablespoons tamari soy sauce
2 tablespoons vegetable oil
1 tablespoon dried minced onion
1 bottle barbecue sauce

1. Trim and cut chicken breasts into cubes a little less than 1 inch square. Thread chicken onto bamboo skewers.

2. In a large baking pan, combine lemon-lime soda, soy sauce, vegetable oil and minced onion, whisking to combine. Place chicken skewers in pan, making sure the marinade covers the chicken. Place in the refrigerator for 2–4 hours.

3. Preheat a barbecue grill to medium hot (about 350 degrees F). Add chicken skewers, cooking for about 6 minutes on each side until meat reaches an internal temperature of 165 degrees F. Use tongs to turn chicken. In the last 2 minutes of cooking, baste the top of each skewer with barbecue sauce. Serve on a platter.

Vegetarian Option: Skewer button mushrooms, green pepper pieces, and pineapple chunks and grill for 5–7 minutes, turning frequently.

★ Makes 8–10 servings

CACTUS KABOBS

1 head iceberg lettuce

2 small cucumbers, sliced

1 pint cherry or grape tomatoes

1 can black olives

Prepared ranch dressing

1. Chop iceberg lettuce into chunks about 2 inches square. Try to keep the layers together. Thread a few chunks of lettuce onto a bamboo skewer.

2. Thread 3 rounds of cucumbers on the skewer, followed by 2 tomatoes and 2 black olives. Serve the cactus kabobs standing upright in a jar or container with ranch dressing on the side.

★ Makes 8–12 servings

SADDLE UP S'MORES

10–12 jumbo-size marshmallows
8 ounces semi-sweet chocolate chips
8–10 graham crackers, crushed

1. Line a baking sheet with wax paper. Place 1 marshmallow on each wooden dowel. Melt chocolate by placing in a microwave-safe bowl and heating for 1 minute on medium power. Remove and stir. Return to the microwave for 30 more seconds on medium before stirring. If needed, continue microwaving in 15-second increments to melt the chocolate.

2. Dip each marshmallow halfway into melted chocolate and roll in crushed graham cracker crumbs. Place on wax paper–covered baking sheet to cool. Tie ribbons around the dowels and serve upright in a jar or container.

★ Makes 10–12 servings

JOHNNY CAKES

1 cup butter, melted

1 cup sugar

4 eggs, beaten

2 cups buttermilk

1 teaspoon baking soda

2 cups cornmeal

2 cups all-purpose flour

1 1/2 teaspoons salt

Honey butter

1. Preheat oven to 375 degrees F. Prepare 6 mini loaf pans with baking spray.

2. Combine butter, sugar and eggs. Add remaining ingredients and stir until just blended. Batter should be lumpy.

3. Pour into prepared mini loaf pans and bake for 25–35 minutes until solid in the center. Serve warm with honey butter.

★ Makes 10–12 servings

Honey Butter

1 cup softened butter

1/2 cup honey

Combine butter with honey and stir to combine.

FIRE-ROASTED COB CORN WITH HERB BUTTER

10 ears sweet corn, husked and washed

Olive oil

Salt to taste

Black pepper to taste

1. Preheat a barbecue grill to medium-low heat (about 325 degrees F).

2. Brush ears of corn with olive oil and sprinkle with salt and pepper to taste. Place corn on grill and cook about 2–3 minutes on each side, rotating to prevent excessive burning for about 8–10 minutes total. Close the grill lid in between rotating. Corn is done when liquid squirts out of the plumped kernels when pressed. Serve with Herb Butter.

(Ears of corn can also be broiled in an oven on a broiler pan or baking sheet about 8 inches from the broiler set on low. Watch carefully and turn the ears frequently, cooking for about 10 minutes total.)

★ Makes 10 servings

Herb Butter

1 cup butter, softened
   (2 cubes)

$^1/_4$ cup fresh sage, chopped

$^1/_4$ cup fresh basil, chopped

$^1/_4$ cup fresh rosemary,
   chopped

Combine all ingredients
and serve with Fire-
Roasted Cob Corn.

REFRESHMENTS

How many treats can you eat in 8 seconds?
Go the distance at the rodeo grounds as you
saddle up to do some serious buckin' with world
champion riders from across the West.

BUCKIN' BULL NACHOS WITH AVOCADO SALSA

1 bag round tortilla chips

2 cups bottled mild salsa

8 ounces cream cheese, softened

2 cups shredded Mexican-style cheese

1. Divide tortilla chips into paper trays or onto small plates.

2. Heat salsa in a microwave for 1–2 minutes on high until hot. Stir in cream cheese and shredded Mexican-style cheese. Cover and return to the microwave to continue heating in 30-second increments, stirring until melted and smooth.

3. Serve melted cheese sauce over chips with Avocado Salsa.

Avocado Salsa

2 avocados, peeled and chopped

2 Roma tomatoes, chopped

2 tablespoons lime juice

1/4 cup fresh cilantro, chopped

1 teaspoon garlic salt (add more to taste)

Combine all ingredients in a small bowl and stir gently. Serve with Buckin' Bull Nachos.

★ Makes 6–8 servings

GET ALONG
PRETZEL DOGGIES

8 beef hot dogs

16 frozen yeast dough rolls, thawed

1 cup baking soda

1 egg, beaten

Kosher salt

Ketchup

Mustard

1. Preheat oven to 425 degrees F. Prepare a baking sheet with nonstick cooking spray.

2. Combine 2 of the thawed dough rounds and stretch into a flat circle about 6 inches across. Place a hot dog in the middle and wrap the dough around the dog, pinching the ends well to seal. Cut 3 slits across the dough, reaching the hot dog on one side. Allow dough to rise for about 30 minutes in a warm place.

3. Fill an 8-quart stock pot about 2/3 full of water. Add baking soda and bring to a boil. As the water boils, add the dough-wrapped hot dogs a few at a time, cooking each for 30 seconds. Remove and shake to drain before placing on the prepared baking sheet. When pretzel dogs are cool enough to handle, insert a corn dog or other wooden stick into each hot dog.

4. Brush each pretzel dog with beaten egg and sprinkle lightly with kosher salt. Bake for 12–15 minutes until a dark golden brown color. Remove from baking sheet and cool on a rack for a few minutes before serving with ketchup and mustard.

Vegetarian Option: Instead of a hot dog, use a cheddar cheese stick. Make sure the dough completely wraps the cheese. For a vegan alternative, try sliced vegetable patties or meatless hot dogs.

★ **Makes 8 servings**

CINNAMON CHURRO SUNDAES

1¹/₂ quarts vanilla bean ice
  cream
3–4 prepared churros
Caramel sauce, warmed
Can of whipped cream
Cinnamon sugar

1. Cut each churro in half and warm on a baking sheet for 5 minutes in an oven at 350 degrees F.

2. In paper cups or serving dishes, place half a churro and add scoops of vanilla bean ice cream.

3. Top with warmed caramel sauce and whipped cream. Sprinkle with cinnamon sugar and serve immediately.

★ Serves 6–8

WHIPPERSNAPPER SLUSH

2 (12-ounce) cans frozen tropical
   fruit juice or punch (choose
   your favorite flavor)
1 liter sparkling or lemon-lime
   soda
Ice

1. In a blender, combine a can
of frozen juice or punch with
half the soda. Fill the rest of
the blender with ice. Blend
well until smooth.

2. Serve with a straw in a
party glass. Repeat with
remaining ingredients.

★ Makes 6–8 servings

JAMBOREE KRISPY POPS

3 tablespoons butter

4 cups mini marshmallows

6 cups Rice Krispies cereal

4 ounces chocolate candy coating (almond bark)

4 ounces white candy coating (almond bark)

4 ounces butterscotch or peanut butter chips

Assorted sprinkles and jimmies

1. Prepare a 13 x 9-inch pan with nonstick cooking spray.

2. In a large microwave-safe bowl, heat the butter and marshmallows on high for 2 minutes and stir. Continue heating for 1 more minute and stir until smooth.

3. Add cereal and stir until well coated. Using buttered hands or a spatula, press cereal mixture into the prepared pan. Allow to cool before cutting into rectangles.

4. Prepare a baking sheet with wax paper. Melt candy coating and chips in microwave in individual bowls on high for 30 seconds before stirring. Continue to microwave in 15-second intervals while stirring to melt.

5. Press wooden sticks into each Rice Krispie rectangle and dip into melted candy coating before decorating with sprinkles. Place on the wax paper baking sheet to cool before serving.

★ Makes 8–12 servings

Chuck Wagon
DINNER

After the last roundup for the season,
it's time for all the 'pokes to gather together
and celebrate with a genuine chuck wagon
dinner. This is a proper feast with fancy
tablecloths and everything.

COOKY'S COLE SLAW

1 head cabbage
1 cup mayonnaise
$^1/_4$ cup sugar
2 tablespoons lemon juice
$^3/_4$ teaspoon salt
Black pepper to taste
1 cup matchstick carrots

1. Roughly cut cabbage through the center to shred and set aside.

2. In a large mixing bowl, combine remaining ingredients except carrots and stir well to mix. Add shredded cabbage and carrots, tossing to mix. Serve immediately or chill.

★ Makes 6–8 servings

TRAIL RIDE BEANS

3 (15-ounce) cans pinto beans
1 small onion, minced
$^{1}/_{4}$ cup brown sugar
$^{1}/_{4}$ cup ketchup
1 tablespoon prepared mustard
1 teaspoon salt
$^{1}/_{2}$ cup crumbled bacon (optional)

1. Preheat oven to 350 degrees F.

2. In a baking dish or small Dutch oven, combine all ingredients and stir well. Bake covered for 25–30 minutes.

★ Makes 6–8 servings

SLOW-COOKED SMOKY BRISKET

3 pounds beef brisket

1 bottle chili sauce

1 (12-ounce) can cola

1 package dry onion soup mix

2 teaspoons liquid natural mesquite smoke flavor

1. In a slow cooker, place brisket fat side up. Pour in the bottle of chili sauce, cola and top with onion soup mix. Drizzle the smoke flavor over everything.

2. Cook on high for at least 90 minutes and on low for 3 hours or more. Before slicing to serve, remove and let stand on a platter covered with aluminum foil for 15 minutes to tenderize. Serve with prepared barbecue sauce if desired.

★ Serves 8–10

CHEDDAR AND HONEY HOT ROCKS

3 cups dry biscuit mix (Bisquick)

1 cup milk

2 tablespoons honey

$1/2$ cup butter, melted

8 ounces cheddar cheese,
   shredded

1. Preheat oven to 450 degrees F. Prepare a baking sheet with parchment paper or nonstick baking spray.

2. Combine all ingredients, stirring to form a soft dough. Let stand for 5 minutes. Turn out dough onto floured surface and knead several times. Roll dough to a half-inch thickness and cut with a small round cookie cutter. Bake at 450 degrees F for 10–12 minutes.

★ Makes 24–30 biscuits

FRESH-SQUEEZED LEMONADE

2$\frac{1}{2}$ cups sugar

2 cups lemon juice (juice of
about 8–10 lemons)

1 (12-ounce) package frozen
raspberries

2 lemons, sliced

Water and ice to make 2 gallons

In a large drink dispenser or
punch bowl, combine sugar,
lemon juice, raspberries and
lemon slices. Add enough
water and ice to make
2 gallons.

★ Makes 2 gallons

The Pioneer's
PANTRY

The rugged pioneers of the Old West built
homes on prairies and in valleys and celebrated
the goodness of the land. Sit down and give
thanks with a proper feast of frontier foods
that are downright delicious.

ORCHARD MEDLEY SALAD

$^1/_2$ cup mayonnaise

4 tablespoons lemon juice

$^1/_2$ teaspoon salt

4 crisp green apples, cored and
  chopped

$^1/_2$ cup candied walnuts

2 cups red grapes

In a mixing bowl, whisk
together mayonnaise and
lemon juice. Add remaining
ingredients and stir gently to
coat.

★ Makes 6 servings

46

POTATOES 'N' COATS

6 russet potatoes
2 eggs, beaten
1/2 cup buttermilk
2 cups bread crumbs
2 teaspoons salt
1 tablespoon dried parsley
1 teaspoon garlic powder
1/2 teaspoon paprika
Black pepper to taste
1/2 cup butter, melted (optional)
Sour cream ranch dip

1. Preheat oven to 425 degrees F. Line a baking sheet with foil. Wash and scrub potatoes. Slice lengthwise into wedges.

2. Combine eggs and buttermilk in a small bowl. In a shallow dish, combine remaining ingredients except butter and sour cream ranch dip. Dredge each wedge in the egg and buttermilk and roll in the breadcrumb mixture. Place on the baking sheet.

3. Bake for 30 minutes until crispy, turning once with a spatula halfway through. If desired, drizzle with melted butter before serving. Serve with sour cream ranch dip.

★ Makes 6–10 servings

OVEN-ROASTED TURKEY WITH KITCHEN GARDEN VEGETABLES

1 (3-pound) precooked oven-roasted turkey breast

5 carrots, sliced

2 onions, halved

1 red bell pepper, seeded and chopped

1 yellow bell pepper, seeded and chopped

1. Preheat oven to 350 degrees F.

2. In a Dutch oven or roasting dish, place the turkey breast and 1 cup of water. Surround with the chopped vegetables and cover.

3. Cook in oven for 60 minutes. Remove and let stand for 10 minutes before serving surrounded by the vegetables.

Vegetarian Option: Instead of turkey, double the vegetables and add whole baby Portobello mushrooms and chopped celery. Season with salt and pepper to taste.

★ Makes 8–10 servings

APPLE TARTS

6 cups Granny Smith apple slices, peeled

3/4 cup sugar

1/2 teaspoon cinnamon

1/4 teaspoon nutmeg

1/4 teaspoon salt

1 refrigerated pie crust

Topping

1/4 cup brown sugar

1/4 cup all-purpose flour

2 tablespoons butter, melted

1/2 cup pecans, chopped

1. Preheat oven to 450 degrees F. Spay a fluted muffin pan with nonstick baking spray.

2. Combine sliced apples in a bowl with sugar, spices and salt. Roll out pie crust and using a round cookie cutter that is larger than the muffin cups, cut out circles of dough. Press dough circles into the muffin cups.

3. Combine all topping ingredients in a bowl and mix. Spoon apples into each muffin cup, on top of crust dough. Add a scoop of topping to each tart. Decorate with cutout of leftover pie crust if desired. Bake for 8–9 minutes until golden brown.

★ Makes 8–10 servings

PIONEER HONEY TAFFY

1 cup sugar
2 tablespoons cornstarch
1/2 teaspoon salt
1/2 cup honey
1 1/2 cups corn syrup
1 cup cream
2 tablespoons butter

1. In a large heavy saucepan, combine the first 3 dry ingredients and stir to mix. Add the honey, corn syrup and cream. Bring to a boil over medium-high heat, stirring to dissolve all the sugar. Once boiling, let mixture cook undisturbed until it reaches 270 degrees F, or soft-crack stage. If you don't have a candy thermometer, drop a spoonful into cold water and it should form threads that, when removed from the water, are flexible, not brittle. Remove from heat and add butter while stirring slowly.

2. Carefully pour hot mixture in a buttered baking sheet. Allow to cool until taffy can be handled. With buttered hands, fold and stretch taffy, continually pulling for 10–15 minutes. This is a great time to have some help. The taffy will lighten in color when it's ready.

3. Form a rope of taffy and cut into 1-inch pieces with a buttered knife or kitchen shears. After cutting, let taffy rest uncovered for about an hour before wrapping in small squares of waxed paper. Tie ribbon on the ends.

WESTERN GRUB

The Wild West was truly a wild place.
With rip roarin' outlaws and bandits lined up
against straight and tall lawmen, you never
knew what might happen at high noon.
So watch your back.

TRAIN ROBBERY GOLD

4 quarts popped popcorn

1 cup brown sugar

$^1/_2$ cup butter or margarine

$^1/_4$ cup corn syrup

$^3/_4$ teaspoon salt

2 teaspoons vanilla

$^1/_2$ teaspoon baking soda

1. Place popcorn in a large brown paper bag and set aside. In a microwave-safe bowl, heat brown sugar, butter, corn syrup, salt and vanilla for 3 minutes. Remove and stir until well blended. Return and cook for another 1^1/2 minutes. Remove and stir in baking soda.

2. Pour hot syrup over popcorn in the paper bag. Close the bag and shake well to coat the popcorn. Place bag in microwave and cook for 30 seconds. Remove and shake. Return to microwave and cook 30 more seconds. Pour out the popcorn onto wax paper and allow to cool.

★ Makes 6–8 servings

BOOT HILL PUDDING CUPS

8 butterscotch pudding cups
2 cups graham cracker crumbs
8 Milano cookies
Decorator gel icing

1. Using a toothpick, decorate the top half of each cookie with the decorator gel icing, creating tombstones.

2. Open pudding cups. Sprinkle graham cracker crumbs generously. Push tombstone cookie into the cup and serve.

★ Makes 8 servings

TEXAS SHEET CAKE

1 cup butter, melted

1 cup hot water

$^1/_4$ cup cocoa

2 cups sugar

2 cups flour

$^1/_4$ teaspoon salt

2 eggs, beaten

1 teaspoon baking soda

1 teaspoon cinnamon (optional)

$^1/_2$ cup sour cream

$1^1/_2$ teaspoons vanilla

Frosting

$^1/_2$ cup butter

$^1/_4$ cup cocoa

$^1/_4$ cup milk

$4^1/_4$ cups powdered sugar (1 pound)

1 teaspoon vanilla

Yellow decorator's icing

1. Preheat oven to 350 degrees F. Spray a half-sheet baking pan with nonstick baking spray.

2. In a large mixing bowl, combine butter, water and cocoa, whisking until smooth. Add remaining ingredients and mix well.

3. Pour into prepared sheet pan and bake for 18–20 minutes until a toothpick inserted in the center comes out clean. Frost while warm. Allow to cool completely and decorate with yellow icing stars.

4. Frosting: In a large saucepan over medium-high heat, bring butter, cocoa and milk to a boil. Add powdered sugar and vanilla and mix with a whisk or electric mixer. Using a spatula, spread over the warm cake.

★ **Makes 10–14 servings**

SHERIFF'S SUGAR COOKIES

2 cups sugar

2 eggs

1 cup shortening, melted

1 cup evaporated milk

2 teaspoons baking powder

1 teaspoon salt

1 teaspoon lemon extract

5½ cups flour

Frosting

3 cups powdered sugar

1 cup butter, softened

1 teaspoon vanilla extract

1–2 tablespoons milk

Gel food coloring (yellow, brown, etc.)

1. Preheat oven to 400 degrees F. Mix together in a large bowl the sugar, eggs, and shortening until smooth and blended. Add evaporated milk, baking powder, salt and lemon extract, stirring well. Mix in flour one cup at a time until dough is stiff and can be formed. Chill dough for at least one hour or cover and refrigerate up to one day.

2. Roll dough on a smooth surface dusted with confectioner's sugar until about $1/2$ inch thick. Using a star-shaped cookie cutter, cut out cookies and place them on an ungreased cookie sheet. You can also use cowboy hat cookie cutters and other western shapes. Bake for 7–9 minutes until puffy and slightly brown on the edges. Cool on a wire rack.

3. Mix together powdered sugar, butter and vanilla for the frosting, whisking until smooth. Add milk a little at a time until desired consistency is reached. Add a little yellow gel food coloring to mixture and stir to combine. Decorate cookies with frosting. Add yellow candies for the tips of the sheriff's star badge.

★ **Makes about 24 cookies**

WILD WEST GINGERBREAD HOUSE

36 full graham cracker sheets plus extras for support

4 pretzel rods

Tootsie Roll candies

Bit o' Honey candies

Box of crackers

Royal Icing

^{1}/$_2$ cup meringue powder (available at cake decorating/craft stores)

1 cup water

8 cups powdered sugar

Gel food coloring (brown, yellow)

1. Make Royal Icing by beating meringue powder and water together until meringue forms stiff peaks, meaning the meringue peaks stand up straight and don't fall over. Mix in powder sugar, one cup at a time, until smooth. Tint as needed with the food coloring.

2. Form the 2 side walls and roof by joining 8 sheets of graham crackers together on the long edges using the Royal Icing as glue. Use pieces of graham cracker to reinforce the joints on the back. After making the side walls, make the front and back walls by "gluing" together 8 graham crackers with frosting on the short ends. These 2 walls will be higher. Using a serrated steak knife, carefully saw out the doorway opening on the bottom of the front wall.

3. On a solid cardboard base, glue together the 4 walls and roof using Royal Icing. Create the windows using Tootsie Rolls and make a sign out of a single full graham cracker with the corners trimmed. Decorate the bottom half first using brown Royal Icing piped on to create wood paneling. Make the swinging doors from 2 pieces of Bit o' Honey candy. Add the overhanging roof made from 2 full graham cracker sheets and support with 4 pretzel rods. Make shingles out of crackers. Draw the sign with a narrow round tip and darker brown icing. For fun, write your name or a message on the sign.

Zac Williams

has been cooking and taking photos since he was a junior wrangler. He is the author of several cookbooks, including *French Fries, Little Monsters Cookbook, Little Aliens Cookbook* and, his newest, *Hungry Campers.* Williams lives in Pleasant View, Utah, with his wife and three little cowpokes.